# CHROMEBOOK FOR SENIORS

## SENIORS

GETTING STARTED WITH CHROME OS

PHIL SHARP

**RIDICULOUSLY**
SIMPLE BOOKS

ANAHEIM, CALIFORNIA

# Contents

Introduction...........................................2

*Tell Me About Accessibility* ........................3

   ACCESSIBILITY FEATURES.............................3

*Tell Me the Basics and Keep It Ridiculously
Simple* ...............................................11

   A WORD (OR PARAGRAPH OR TWO) ABOUT CHROME
OS ....................................................11

   THE KEYBOARD .....................................12

*All About Chrome OS* ...............................15

   USER ACCOUNTS.....................................17

   SETTINGS OVERVIEW.................................18

*Getting Around the OS* .............................21

   DESKTOP ..........................................22

   THE LAUNCHER AND CHROME SHELF ...............22

   CHROME WINDOWS...................................23

   FILES AND GOOGLE DRIVE ..........................24

   OFFLINE ...........................................24

*All About Chrome OS* ...............................26

   THE CHROME BROWSER.............................27

   ANATOMY OF A GOOGLE CHROME WINDOW ........28

   TABS AND WINDOWS ...............................29

   BROWSING INCOGNITO ............................31

   BOOKMARKS .......................................32

   RECENT AND HISTORY .............................34

   GOOGLE CHROME AND YOUR GOOGLE ACCOUNT ..35

   STORED PASSWORDS................................35

   FORM AUTOFILL ...................................37

   CHROME EXTENSIONS...............................37

THE CHROME WEB STORE......................37

APPS ...............................................39

EXTENSIONS .....................................39

THEMES............................................40

INSTALLING NEW CHROME CONTENT ...............41

MANAGING APPS, EXTENSIONS AND THEMES........42

*There's a Pre-Installed App for That* .............*44*

GOOGLE DOCS.....................................45

GOOGLE SHEETS..................................50

GOOGLE SLIDES ..................................51

SCRATCHPAD ....................................52

GOOGLE+ AND HANGOUTS..........................52

GMAIL ............................................57

YOUTUBE .........................................67

CALCULATOR .....................................73

CAMERA ..........................................74

CHROME REMOTE DESKTOP.........................75

GOOGLE+ PHOTOS ................................76

GOOGLE KEEP ....................................77

GOOGLE MAPS AND GOOGLE MY MAPS ..............78

GOOGLE FORMS....................................82

GOOGLE DRAWINGS ...............................83

PLAY MUSIC, PLAY BOOKS, AND PLAY MOVIES ......83

GOOGLE CALENDAR................................86

*Making It Your Own With Customizations* .......*89*

CHANGING THE APPEARANCE .........................91

DEVICE.............................................92

SEARCHING .......................................95

PEOPLE ....................................96

DATE AND TIME ..........................97

PRIVACY ...................................97

WEB CONTENT ...........................99

LANGUAGES ..............................99

DOWNLOADS .............................100

HTTPS/SSL CERTIFICATES .............101

GOOGLE CLOUD PRINT.................101

STARTUP..................................101

POWERWASH AND RESET .............102

SUPERVISED ACCOUNTS...............103

TROUBLESHOOTING AND MAINTAINING YOUR
CHROMEBOOK ..........................104

Appendix A: Specs ....................108

Appendix B: Shortcut Keys .......110

Popular shortcuts.....................110

All other shortcuts ...................111

OS - Operating System.

URL -

Reboot = close app & reopen

# INTRODUCTION

Chromebooks are perfect for Seniors. Hopefully you are at a state in your life where the Internet helps you but doesn't define you.

You don't need to have a powerhouse computer that can have 200 spreadsheets running at the same time or watching a movie while you have 100 other apps open!

You just want a computer that lets you check up on things, and maybe stream a movie or to. In a word: something simple.

If that sounds like you, then all you have to do is figure out how to use a Chromebook! Fortunately, if you've ever used the Internet, then that part will come pretty easy.

This book will walk you through what you need to know so you can be up and running in no time.

Ready? Let's get started!

# [1]

# TELL ME ABOUT ACCESSIBILITY

This chapter will cover:
*   How to make Chrome easier to see, hear, and use!

## ACCESSIBILITY FEATURES

We are going to do things a little backwards. Normally, I start these books with a crash course of features, but for this book, I'm going to cover accessibility features first. Accessibility features enhance the experience for users who might have trouble seeing, hearing, or just don't know how fast the mouse pad feels.

Why?

Because there's a lot of features that might be helpful to you as you learn--such as text to speech.

To get started, open up Chrome.

It's this button on the bottom of your screen:

Once it's open, look to the right hand side just below the X. See the three dots? Click that.

That brings up a drop down menu. You'll want to go to the bottom to the Settings option. Click that when you get there.

Edit                    Cut        Copy        Paste

Settings

This brings up the settings menu. What you
want is the three lines on the left hand side. When
you click that, it will bring up another menu.

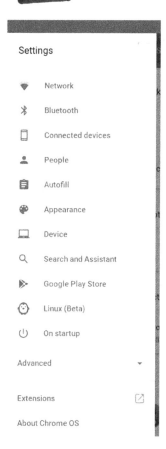

Settings

- ▼  Network
- ✳  Bluetooth
- ☐  Connected devices
- ▲  People
- ☰  Autofill
- ⬤  Appearance
- ▭  Device
- ⚲  Search and Assistant
- ▶  Google Play Store
- ☺  Linux (Beta)
- ⏻  On startup

Advanced        ▼

Extensions      ⬀

About Chrome OS

Go all the way to the bottom and click advanced. Don't worry! This won't be advanced! And we are going to come back to cover the settings menu thoroughly once we go over some other parts of the computer you need to know.

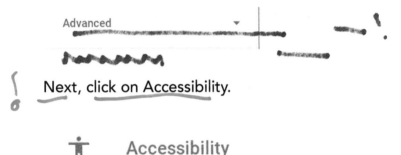

Next, click on Accessibility.

This brings up the accessibility menu. See! Doesn't look too complicated does it?!

Accessibility

Always show accessibility options in the system menu

Manage accessibility features
Enable accessibility features

Reset settings

Restore settings to their original defaults

Powerwash
Remove all user accounts and reset your Google Chrome device to be just like new.

The bottom part we'll cover letter. That's just about resetting everything, which you don't want to do right now--probably never. The part we want to click next is Manage accessibility features.

Manage accessibility features
Enable accessibility features

This brings up a whole slew of features. For the most part, these will all be toggles--which means *on* you click it to turn it on and click it again to turn it *off* off.

*First* → The first is Text-to-Speech. Text-to-Speech will read back text (like emails and documents) to you. The first two options turn it on and the last lets you edit things like how loud it is.

Text-to-Speech →

Enable ChromeVox (spoken feedback)

Enable select-to-speak
Hear text read aloud

Text-to-Speech voice settings
Select and customize text-to-speech voices

Next is display. This lets you turn on high contrast if you're having a hard time seeing your screen; you can also make everything bigger by turning on the zoom. *bigger*

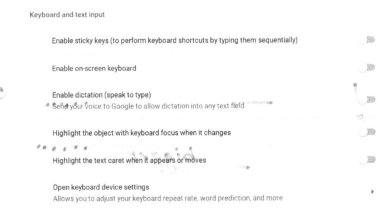

Display

Use high contrast mode

Enable fullscreen magnifier

Fullscreen zoom level:        Custom

Enable docked magnifier

Docked zoom level:        4x

Open display device settings
Allows you to adjust your screen resolution

Open appearance settings
Customize your text size

Next up is keyboard settings. If you are not a fan of typing, then you'll love this area--one of the options is dictation--or speak to type; say what you want and it will appear on your screen.

Keyboard and text input

Enable sticky keys (to perform keyboard shortcuts by typing them sequentially)

Enable on-screen keyboard

Enable dictation (speak to type)
Send your voice to Google to allow dictation into any text field.

Highlight the object with keyboard focus when it changes

Highlight the text caret when it appears or moves

Open keyboard device settings
Allows you to adjust your keyboard repeat rate, word prediction, and more

If you aren't a fan of the touchpad, you aren't alone. A lot of people have difficulty getting used to it. This can adjust the size you see on the screen--so it's easier to find. You can also turn on highlighting, which means it appears slightly highlighted on your screen. The last setting lets you change the overall speed and other settings-- so if it's too quick when you drag your finger on it, you can adjust the responsiveness.

Mouse and touchpad

Automatically click when the mouse cursor stops

Show large mouse cursor

Highlight the mouse cursor when it's moving

Open mouse and touchpad device settings
Allows you to enable/disable tap-to-click and tap dragging

Finally, the Audio is pretty straightforward. It changes the sound from the stereo (surround sound) to mono (same sound on all speakers); you can also pick if you want sound at startup.

Audio

Play the same audio through all speakers (mono audio)

Play sound on startup

Add additional features
Open Chrome Web Store

# [2]

# TELL ME THE BASICS AND KEEP IT RIDICULOUSLY SIMPLE

This chapter will cover:
- What's Chrome OS
- The Keyboard

A WORD (OR PARAGRAPH OR TWO) ABOUT CHROME OS

For years, Google has taken what you could call the "Apple approach" to computers and tablets. Computers ran Chrome and tablets ran Android (e.g. iPads run iOS and MacBooks run MacOS). Like iPads and Macbooks, there were similarities between Android tablets and Chrome computers. But there were also differences.

The Pixel Slate breaks this tradition by running the same operating system (OS) that you are familiar with if you have a Chromebook. What's more, newer Chromebooks can also download Android apps. That means if there's an app you love on your phone, you can use it on your computer as well.

THE KEYBOARD

The layout of the keyboard isn't completely different from other computers, but there are a few keys you might not be familiar with. The list below is an overview of those keys. Because there are so many different Chromebook models, this list will vary, so the following is just a reference.

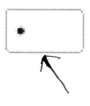
Searches all the apps installed on your computer as well as the web. This button is where the Caps Lock key normally is—to use Caps Lock, hit this button and the Alt key at the same time.

Launches the Google Assistant (Google's version of Siri).

| | |
|---|---|
| ← | Goes to the previous page in your browser history. |
| C | Reloads your current page. |
| ⟦⟧ | This puts your current application in full screen mode; all the tabs and the launcher will be hidden. |
| ▯▮ | Shows all windows in Overview mode. |
| ◌ | Dim the screen. (F5) |
| ○ | Make the screen brighter. (F6) |
| ▶‖ | Play/pause (F7) |
| 🔇 | Mute (F8) |
| ◀ | Lower the volume. (F9) |
| ◀)) | Raise the volume. (F10) |
| ≡ | Open your status area (where your account picture appears). |

# [3]

# ALL ABOUT CHROME OS

This chapter will cover:
- User accounts
- Settings overview

Chrome OS is a very close relative of Google's Internet browser, Google Chrome. As the owner of a Chromebook, you'll quickly see that Chrome is about to become a very big part of your life. This is a good thing; it's a fast, easy-to-use web browser with all kinds of features and seemingly unlimited potential for enhancement thanks to apps and extensions available in the Chrome Web Store. The Chrome browser means so much more than just web browsing in Chrome OS though, due to the fact that almost every app you run in Chrome OS runs inside a Chrome browser window. Don't worry if that sounds bizarre at first—you'll get the hang of it quickly and we'll walk you through everything you need to know!

The Chrome Web Store contains products that are similar enough to major desktop applications that you'll hardly be able to tell the difference. As a bonus, many of them are completely free (and if you've ever shelled out for Photoshop, we know that's going to come as a relief!).

Since most of Chromebook's functionality happens within a browser, Chromebook users can get to the majority of their Chromebook work from any computer with the free Google Chrome browser installed. Google's cloud storage system—Google Drive—is baked into Chrome OS and steadily saves your work as you go. As long as you're connected to wi-fi, if catastrophe strikes your physical Chromebook, your important files and documents are safe and sound in the cloud.

If you're scratching your head at this point, don't worry. Chromebook is easy to use, and the best way to understand it is to turn the thing on, roll up your sleeves, and dive right in. And we're going to do just that in the next chapter!

## USER ACCOUNTS

One of the best features about any Chromebook is the ability to add user accounts; unlike other computers, you can take all of your settings with you. So let's say you have a Chromebook, and log in to another Chromebook. All of your apps, settings, customizations are there waiting for you. It's almost like you are using your personal computer even though you are logged in as a guest. This also means when you get another computer in the future, it's very simple to set up. Just log in and you are done!

Having multiple accounts also makes it very easy to share a computer in your household. From the login screen, you can either add a user or log in as a guest. Anyone who has a Google account (if you have Gmail then you have one—if you don't have Gmail you might have one without knowing it, as this is what many businesses use), can set up an account on your computer. Don't worry: this won't give other users access to any of your files or personal settings.

There is only one important thing to remember with regard to user accounts: set up the device owner first! If you use another account to sign into the computer for the first time, then that's the device owner and the person who will have administrator rights that other users won't have. There's no way to transfer ownership to another user, so you would have to reset your computer if that happens.

SETTINGS OVERVIEW

We'll discuss the settings a little further throughout this book, but there are a few settings you'll want to know about right now.

## User Accounts

If you want to disable people from being able to log in to your settings, then log in to your account, click on your user profile image (bottom right corner of the screen), then click the settings button:

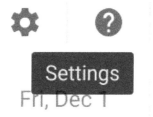

From here, you'll be taken to a browser window with a list of some of the most common settings. Scroll to the bottom of the list and click the button labeled "Manage Other Users." By default, everything is toggled on; click it once to toggle it off. Hit the back button and it saves your settings automatically.

*1x off*

## Keyboard Settings

The location of the Alt key on a computer keyboard is what a Mac user might use as the Command key. There are several keys like this. You can either retrain your mind or you can go into the keyboard settings and change the shortcuts around a little. In the settings you can also change things like the language.

## Touchpad Settings

Mac users will be a little annoyed with scrolling on their new computer! That's because the scrolling on an Apple device is the opposite of scrolling on the Chromebook! Again, you can either retrain your mind or you can just change the setting. "Australian" is the scrolling you will want. Another setting you will probably want to change is the Touchpad speed; to some users, it might feel a little laggy. It's an easy fix. Just slide the Touchpad speed button to the right for a faster scroll.

# [4]

# GETTING AROUND THE OS

This chapter will cover:
- The Desktop
- Launcher and Chrome Shelf
- Chrome Windows
- Files and Google Drive
- Offline Mode

Google's OS seems much like a marriage between Windows OS and Mac OS, and that's a good thing, because with very little instruction, everything will start feeling natural. In this section, you'll get a crash course in the basic features of the OS and where things are located.

DESKTOP

Your desktop takes up the bulk of the screen. It includes a desktop wallpaper image, which can be customized, and you can also store files and shortcuts here for easy access, just like other desktops. Chances are, however, you'll probably find yourself not making much use of the Desktop space. Chrome's intuitive interface makes it easier just to store everything in your Google Drive. I've used Chrome OS for many years, and I find the desktop is usually just a place to put a pretty picture.

THE LAUNCHER AND CHROME SHELF

The Launcher button is similar to the Start button on a Windows computer—only a bit simpler. Clicking on the Launcher button will reveal every app associated with your Google account. This apps menu does extend to the right, and you may need to use the horizontal page indicator icons at the bottom of the menu to move from screen to screen.

SHELF= Taskbar = SHORTCUTS

Next to the Apps button, you'll find your Chrome "shelf." You might be used to thinking of this area as a taskbar or dock, but in Chrome, it's called the shelf. The shelf contains shortcuts to your favorite apps and documents, and lets you know what's currently running. In the screenshot above, you can see that we're currently running the Chrome browser, gmail, the app HipChat, and the Files app, due to the small gray dot under those icons.

To the far right (where your photo is) is the Systems Tray Menu; this is where you'll see settings, apps that have updated, and battery life.

CHROME WINDOWS

Chrome is almost entirely browser based; there are a few more traditional looking apps (like Google Hangouts), but most of the apps you see on your Chrome Shelf are more like shortcuts to a web page. I'll explain the apps that come with the Chromebook and how to get additional ones later in this book.

## FILES AND GOOGLE DRIVE

Every computer has "local" storage—which is all the stuff (files, photos, documents) that are stored directly on the computer; Windows computers have File/System Explorer; Mac Computers have Finder; and Chrome computers have Files. Chrome computers have one extra storage drive: Google Drive. Google Drive is cloud-based, which means whatever you store there will be available on the Internet (privately unless you make it public). This makes it easy to store a file that you want to use on another computer. The Files app shows you both local files (on your computer) and cloud files (stored online). If you were to connect a USB storage device like a flash drive or an external hard drive, you'd see that in Files as well.

Keep in mind that Google Drive is not unlimited storage; your Google account has 15GB of free storage. After that, it's $1.99 a month and up. It's a very inexpensive solution, and one you should consider for backing up files you store on your computer. Also, buying any new Chromebook may mean you are qualified for free storage. You can see Google's current offerings here: https://www.google.com/chromebook/offers/

## OFFLINE

The Chromebook is designed to be used online. That said, the Internet is not required. Even Google's suite of online apps (Docs, Sheets, and

Slides) can be used offline. If you plan to work on a Google Doc file (or Sheets/Slides) make sure you move it into the offline folder before logging off.

# [5]

# ALL ABOUT CHROME OS
*Operating System*

This chapter will cover:
- Anatomy of the Chrome Window
- Tabs and Windows
- Incognito
- Bookmarks
- History
- Passwords
- Autofill
- Chrome Extensions
- Web Store and Apps
- Installing and Managing Chrome Content

## THE CHROME BROWSER

The web browser that comes standard with your Chromebook is, for all intents and purposes, the very same version of Chrome that's available for Windows, OSX, and Linux computers. So if you're already using Chrome on another device, then there's very little learning curve. One thing you'll love right away is all of your bookmarks and settings will be carried over from one device to the next. There are still a few things you'll want to know about, so I'll cover them here.

You'll notice that opening Chrome doesn't automatically put the browser into full-screen mode. You can resize Chrome window two different ways—by pressing the green maximize button or by tapping the three dots in the top right corner and then tapping the full-screen button next to the zoom options.

If you're using Chrome on other devices, you'll be able to access all of your currently open pages and bookmarks by clicking "Other Devices," (click the three dots, hover over "history," and scroll to the bottom of the list). If you've accidentally closed a web page, Chrome will save it for a period of time under the "Recently Closed" menu.

## ANATOMY OF A GOOGLE CHROME WINDOW

Chrome stays out of your way, for the most part. The vast majority of a Chrome window is reserved for content—whether it's a web page, a Google Docs document, a game, or any other Chrome app.

Everything you need to manage a Chrome window is located at the top of the page. At the top right corner, you'll see the Back, Forward and Refresh buttons. These are used to navigate back or forward through your recent screen views and to reload a page. They match up with the three keys on the keyboard directly to the right of the ESC key on the top row.

In the center of the top part of the screen, you'll see the address/search bar, known as the Chrome "omnibox." Type a website's address (google.com, facebook.com) here to go directly to that site. You can also use this area as a search bar ("kittens," "DIY birdhouse," etc.).

<!-- address bar image -->
🔒 https://www.google.com                                    ☆

At the right end of the omnibox, you'll see a star. Click that star to bookmark the web page (we'll go into more detail on this process in just a second).

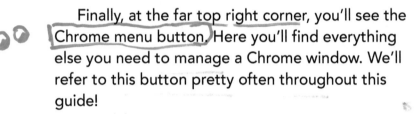

Finally, at the far top right corner, you'll see the Chrome menu button. Here you'll find everything else you need to manage a Chrome window. We'll refer to this button pretty often throughout this guide!

## TABS AND WINDOWS

There are two viewing units to be aware of in Chrome—tabs and windows. Tabs open inside one window, as pictured below. You can open a new tab by pressing CTRL+T (remember: t for tab), by right-clicking the Chrome icon in the shelf, or by clicking

 > New Tab.

Opening a page in a new window, on the other hand, opens a completely separate frame (which

*open new windows*

can then be populated with a new group of tabs, if you like). You can open new windows by pressing CTRL+N (N for new), by right-clicking the Chrome

icon on the shelf, or by clicking ☰ > New Window.

When tabs were first introduced, they streamlined the laborious process of switching between several windows while browsing the Internet. As a result, many users now associate tabs with easier workflow. However, on a Chromebook, it's often easier to switch between windows than between tabs, thanks to the Window Switch key on the top row. Pressing the Window Switch key reveals every open window, giving you the title and a visual preview of each one. Keep this in mind when you're formulating your workflow windows/tabs strategy!

## BROWSING INCOGNITO

If you're shopping for birthday presents, or doing anything else that you don't want enshrined in your search history, Incognito is the browsing mode for you. Pages you view while in an Incognito tab won't be saved in your history. Search terms won't resurface in your search history, and website cookies won't be stored on your computer. However, if you download or bookmark anything, remember that it will be retained on your system.

To open an Incognito tab in Chrome, press CTRL+SHIFT+N, right-click the Chrome icon on the shelf, or click ≡ > New Window. You can tell at a glance which windows are Incognito by looking for the shadowy figure in sunglasses peeking from behind the top left corner.

BOOKMARKS

Bookmarks are a handy way to organize your favorite sites for fast access later on. There are a few different ways to bookmark a site. You can click the Star outline in the omnibox, as previously discussed, or you can press CTRL+D. You can also

navigate to  > Bookmarks > Bookmark this page.

By default, your bookmarks are stored in the bookmarks bar, which is not visible by default. The bookmarks bar, when enabled, appears underneath the omnibox. To display the bookmarks bar, click

> Bookmarks > Show bookmarks bar, or press CTRL+SHIFT+B. To hide it, follow the same path or use the same keyboard shortcut.

If you don't like the automatic wording for each bookmark, you can easily edit it, either when adding the bookmark or later by managing your bookmarks. To manage bookmarks, right-click the bookmark and then click Edit (or Delete, or

whatever you need to do). Then click > Bookmarks > Bookmark Manager, or press CTRL+SHIFT+O. Inside the bookmark manager, you can right-click bookmarks to edit them, as pictured below. You can also rearrange the order of your bookmarks either in the Bookmark Manager or by dragging them around on the bookmarks bar itself. The most common edit we make for bookmarks is shortening the name in order to fit as many as possible in our bookmarks bar!

Of course, you may eventually run out of room in the bookmarks bar. If this happens, a double arrow will appear at the end of the bookmark bar. Clicking the arrow will reveal the rest of your bookmarks. This may be enough for you, but if you'd like a better way of managing large numbers of bookmarks, we recommend organizing your bookmarks into folders. To do this, open the Bookmark Manager (CTRL+SHIFT+O). Click the Folders heading on the left, and then click Add folder.

You can add as many folders as you like. Once the folders are added, you can drag your bookmarks into them in the Bookmarks Manager. You can either display your folders on the bookmarks bar or organize them in the Other

Bookmarks folder, which you can get to at >
Bookmarks.

Don't forget that in Chrome OS, practically
everything you look at is going to be a web page.
This means that you can set up bookmarks for
Google Docs documents, Google Slides
presentations, games, etc. It's a great way to
organize a project as well as a way to organize your
favorite websites.


RECENT AND HISTORY

Chrome stores your recently viewed pages and
full browsing history to make it easy to get back to
places you've already been. You can see your

recently closed tabs at > Recent. This is a
lifesaver if you accidentally close a tab!

You'll find your full browsing history at >
History or by pressing CTRL+H (H for history). To
clear your history at any time, visit your History and
then click Clear browsing data. You can either
delete history from the past hour, day, week,
month, or, as Google so poetically phrases it, the
beginning of time. You can also specify what kind
of history you want to delete. For example, you can
delete your list of recently visited sites, but retain
any passwords you've saved in Chrome.

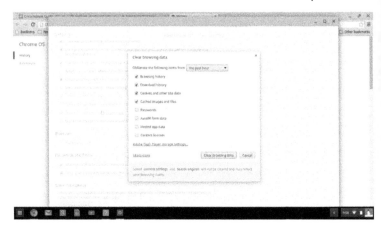

## GOOGLE CHROME AND YOUR GOOGLE ACCOUNT

When you set up a new Chromebook, your system will automatically sign you in to the Google Chrome browser. You can sign into Chrome from other computers as well, though. Signing in to Chrome will allow you to see your browsing history from other Chrome sessions on other computers, your stored passwords, your extensions, and more. To sign into Chrome, click Sign in at the top right corner of a Chrome browser window.

## STORED PASSWORDS

Google Chrome will offer to remember passwords for you whenever you enter them into a website. A popup box will ask you if you want to save the password. You can say Nope to dismiss the box once, or you can click the arrow next to Nope for the Never for this site option.

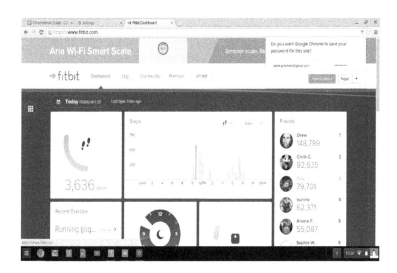

Any passwords you save on your Chromebook or Slate will actually be associated with your Google account. This means that you can use them any time you sign into Chrome, on any computer (though we recommend avoiding signing in on public computers, just to be safe).

If you need to manage your stored passwords, visit ≡ > Settings. At the bottom of the Settings screen, click Show advanced settings. Scroll down until you see the Passwords and Forms heading. Underneath it, click Manage passwords. Here, you can edit or delete your stored passwords. You can also deselect Offer to save your web passwords if you don't want Chrome to store any passwords for you.

Passwords and forms

- ☑ Enable Autofill to fill out web forms in a single click.  Manage Autofill settings
- ☑ Offer to save your web passwords.  Manage passwords

## FORM AUTOFILL

Form Autofill handles forms that you repeatedly fill in. It can remember your name, address, phone number, email address, etc. It's useful for repeated data entry, but you may occasionally need to manage your Autofill settings if you move or change your phone number. To do so, visit Settings > Passwords and forms and click Manage Autofill settings.

## CHROME EXTENSIONS

Extensions extend Chrome's functionality in all kinds of ways, and the enormous range of free extensions to choose from is a huge part of what makes Google Chrome so great. We'll share some of our favorites later in Part 5, and you can explore on your own in the Web Store, which we'll cover next.

## THE CHROME WEB STORE

You'll want to get to know the Web Store sooner rather than later, since it's where you'll find new apps and extensions for your Chromebook. Fortunately, this "Store" has an enormous free section in it, so tricking out your Chromebook won't necessarily break the bank!

You'll find the Web Store by clicking the Apps button in the lower left corner. If you're an Android user, be aware that the Chrome Web Store isn't exactly the same thing as the Google Play Store, though there's a lot of duplicated content.

There are three big categories in the Store— apps, extensions, and themes. You can choose which broad category you're interested in at the top of the Web Store navigation panel on the left.

Before jumping in, it's worth noting here a very big feature added to both the Chromebook and all new Chromebooks: The Android store!

Why is that important? All those apps that you've already downloaded on your Android tablet or phone can now be downloaded on your computer. It also turns your Chromebook into a tablet. You can download any app from the Play Store and it will install on your computer (play.google.com).

## APPS

The apps section of the store contains two types of apps—Chrome apps and website apps. Website "apps" are basically bookmarks. These are websites that you can visit anywhere from any computer, generally with any browser. They're usually free. Chrome apps, on the other hand, make modifications to your Chrome browser in order to function. You will need to be running Chrome in order to use them, and they will need to be installed on the copy of Chrome you're using. This distinction is largely academic for most users. Whether an app is a web app or a Chrome app, adding it to your Chromebook will mean that it appears in your Apps button menu and that it can be pinned to your shelf.

Store apps can be browsed by category, using the dropdown menu under Categories in the left menu. You can also search by feature, like "runs offline" (meaning that the app doesn't require an Internet connection to function), by Google, Free, and Available for Android (very useful if you want to keep your Chromebook and Android smartphone or tablet closely in sync). Finally, you can also sort by the average star rating.

## EXTENSIONS

Unlike apps, extensions allow you to do more with every page you visit in Chrome. Extensions let you do more with the Chrome browser, and there are all kinds of possibilities out there. There are extensions that convert currency on webpages for you, help you pin images to your Pinterest boards, generate secure passwords, or help you manage your online privacy.

Like apps, extensions can be narrowed down by category, special features (including Free), and star rating.

THEMES

Themes are similar to desktop wallpaper, but instead of decorating your desktop, they decorate the Chrome window itself. Themes change the appearance of an empty window, typically by showing an image or pattern, and altering the color of the outer edges of the window. In the example below, we've enabled a dark theme.

We freely admit that while apps and extensions make us salivate, we're not quite as enamored with Chrome theming. We're usually in too much of a hurry to get to our websites, content, and apps to appreciate them. Your mileage may vary, though, and it's not a bad idea to browse some of the free themes in the Store to see if any strike your fancy.

## INSTALLING NEW CHROME CONTENT

Installing a new app, extension, or theme is incredibly simple, especially if it's free. To install free content, simply click the FREE text from a search result, and then click the Add to Chrome button that appears on the content's information screen.

If an app, extension, or theme costs money, click the Buy for… button.

Then click Add. At this point, if you haven't already set up Google Wallet, you'll be prompted to do so. Google Wallet is simply Google's credit card manager. Add a payment method as prompted, and Google will save that information for later. You can add more than one payment method if you prefer. From there, confirm the purchase, and your new paid app, extension, or theme will be installed for you.

## MANAGING APPS, EXTENSIONS AND THEMES

After you've started amassing a library of apps, extensions and themes, you may occasionally need to temporarily disable or delete them. You can manage your apps by clicking the Apps button and then right-clicking the app you'd like to delete or alter.

Extensions are a little more complicated. You can find your extensions under ☰ > More Tools > Extensions, or under ☰ > History (alternately, press CTRL+H). On the History screen, click Extensions on the left. This will display a list of every installed extension on your system.

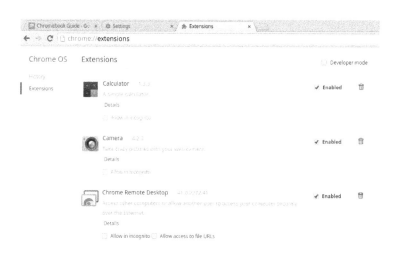

Note that you can disable extensions by deselecting the Enabled checkbox (a good temporary measure), or you can click the trashcan icon to permanently delete something.

# [6]

# THERE'S A PRE-INSTALLED APP FOR THAT

This chapter will cover:
- Google Docs, Sheets, Slides
- Scratchpad
- Google+ Hangouts
- Gmail
- YouTube
- Calculator
- Camera
- Chrome Remote Desktop
- Photos
- Keep
- Google Maps and Google My Maps
- Google Forms
- Drawings
- Play Music, Play Books, and Play Movies
- Google Calendar
- Google Play
- 

Just like any computer, your Chromebook will have apps installed right out of the box. Here is an overview and what they're good for.

GOOGLE DOCS

Google Docs, briefly, is Google's version of Microsoft Word or Apple Pages. You can edit a document just like you would in any other processor, but it's all online and synced automatically, which means it's very difficult to lose anything. You can also share documents and collaborate in real time.

Docs really shines through its connection to Google Drive. Anything you start in Google Docs is automatically saved in your Google Drive account —no need to worry about losing work through power failures, device catastrophes, or really just about any other scenario. Changes are saved as you go, and so are versions, so it's easy to revert to an earlier stage of a draft if you need to.

The main Docs menu consists of File, Edit, Insert, Format, Tools, Table, Add-ons, and Help. Each of these menu items contains a dropdown menu full of features. The full power of Docs is beyond the scope of this guide, but we'll show you some of the basics.

### Starting a New Google Doc

To start a new document, simply open Docs for the first time, or click File > New to open a new document. Notice that Google Docs > File > New will also let you start new Sheets, Slides, Drawings, or Forms projects as well.

### Saving a Google Doc

Google Docs saves everything as you go so you'll rarely need to save manually. You can find the status of your file to the right of the menu if you're concerned. Google Docs does save your work offline as well, so if you're not connected to Drive, you won't lose your work and you can verify that Chromebook has saved it for you.

All changes saved in Drive

All changes saved offline

Formatting a Google Doc

You'll find all the standard text editing options you'd expect in the top menu area, including font size, typeface, bold, italic, underline, text color, hyperlinks, and text alignment. If that doesn't cover you, though, you'll also find spacing, lists, indent control, and format clearing under More.

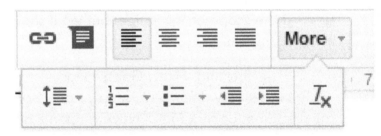

Collaborating Using Google Docs

Google Docs is hands-down one of the easiest ways to work on a group document. To invite people to share your Doc, click the blue Share button in the top right corner (note that hovering over this button will also give you the current shared status of your Doc).

You can add existing Google contacts by entering their names, or you can invite anyone through their email address. Note that your collaborators will need to set up a free Google Account to use Google Drive. You can choose the level of access you want collaborators to have—they can edit, comment, or merely view your shared document. You can remove them at any time by using the Share button again.

When two or more people are editing a document at the same time, you'll be able to see that person's cursor position and watch edits in real time. If you're concerned about losing work, remember that Google Docs saves version history for you, so it's easy to revert if you need to. Click File > See revision history (or press CTRL+ALT+SHIFT+G). By default, revisions are shown grouped into daily periods, but if you want to see changes made by the minute, click "Show more detailed revisions" at the bottom of the revisions panel. You can see which collaborator made each change in a group document. Of course, the slightly less elegant Undo and Redo functions are always available as well!

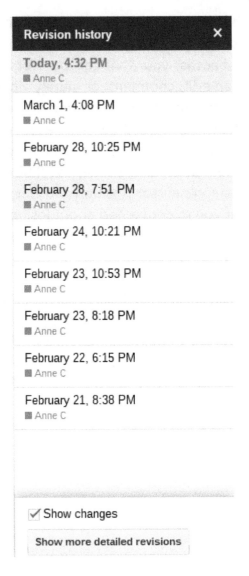

Dealing with Other File Formats
Fortunately, you can edit Microsoft Office files
in Google apps like Google Docs. Just open the file
and edit away. Google Docs can also open files
with .ODT, .DOT, .HTML, and .TXT file extensions,

though there's always a chance that the original formatting may not survive the conversion entirely intact.

## Add-ons

Most of the Google productivity apps include the ability to add on functionality, typically designed by third party developers. You can search for add-ons by clicking the Add-ons menu item at the top of the screen. Click Get add-ons to start searching for the additional functions you need. For example, in Docs, you can install add-ons that reveal the document's structure in a table of contents presentation in the sidebar. There's even a Sudoku add-on for Sheets!

## GOOGLE SHEETS

Google Sheets is Google's answer to Microsoft Excel. If you're familiar with any spreadsheet program, you should feel pretty at home in Sheets. Like almost every other spreadsheet program, Google Sheets will do all the heavy lifting for you when it comes to calculations. Entering formulas in Google Sheets is reasonably similar to Excel. Just type = at the beginning of a cell and then fill in your formula. Of course, there are some minor syntactical differences you'll need to get the hang of, but it's nothing too difficult. Sheets will help you build your formulas by giving you input examples, and you can create charts from your data and define custom sorting and filtering rules.

## GOOGLE SLIDES

Google Slides is a presentation app, like Microsoft PowerPoint. Slides includes several prepackaged presentation themes to get you started, or you can begin with a blank slate. Your completed presentation can be downloaded as a PowerPoint, PDF, image, scalable vector graphic or plain text file, making Slides presentations compatible with just about any environment. There's also a very useful "Publish to the web" feature available in the File menu that will generate a public URL that you can share with your colleagues and/or the entire world. You can also embed Slides presentations in web pages or blog posts. To do this go to File and Publish to the Web.

Publish to the web
⨯

This document is not published to the web.

Make your content visible to anyone by publishing it to the web. You can link to or embed your document. Learn more

**Link**   Embed

**Auto-advance slides:**

every 3 seconds (default ⬍

☐ Start slideshow as soon as the player loads

☐ Restart the slideshow after the last slide

Publish

▸ Published content & settings

## SCRATCHPAD

Scratchpad is meant for small, simple document creation (like Notes on Mac or Notepad on Windows). Things like grocery and to-do lists that don't necessarily need advanced formatting or structure for later publishing work well with Scratchpad.

## GOOGLE+ AND HANGOUTS

Google+ began life as Google's attempt at a social network. It was their answer to Facebook and Twitter. If you are reading this wondering what is Google+ then you probably can tell they didn't quite accomplish everything they hoped. It will, in fact, be discontinued shortly.

Google+ has been out for over six years, which may surprise you. It certainly isn't Google's most widely used product, but it has grown in popularity since it came out and has evolved a lot. Sharing photos, videos, and more are made possible through the network. For businesses, the most important feature is Hangouts—a Skype-like service that lets you have group video calls and share screens.

To sign up for Google+, you'll first need to enter your name, gender, and birthday. Next, Google+ will suggest people you may know, based on any existing Gmail contacts you've entered. Use the Add button to add them to your circles (in Google+ you'll organize your contacts into circles, like friends, college buddies, frenemies, etc.).

Next, Google+ will suggest some topics for you to follow that you might be interested in. Finally, you'll be able to update your profile by adding a photo and some additional personal details. Then you'll be all set to start using Google+!

**Put a face to your name**
Update your public profile and photo.

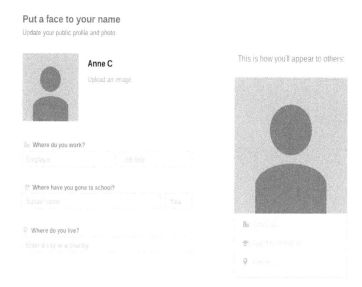

Anne C
Upload an image

This is how you'll appear to others:

Where do you work?
Employer          Job title

Where have you gone to school?
School name          Year

Where do you live?
Enter a city or a country

Inside the Google+ app, there are a few things to be aware of. In the top left corner, you'll see a button labeled Home. Click this button to expand the Google+ menu.

Google+     Se

⌂ Home

🧑 Profile

👥 People

🎡 Photos

---

🎡 Communities

🗓 Events

💬 Hangouts

🔲 Pages

📍 Local

⚙ Settings

Feedback · Tour
Help · Region

This menu should be familiar to Facebook users. You'll see options to get to your profile and edit it if necessary, as well as links to the people you follow and the photos you've posted. You'll also find Communities, Events, Hangouts, Pages, Local info, and Settings.

### Posting in Google+

You can post various items in Google+, just like Facebook. You can add text, photos, links, videos, events (which you can invite your contacts to, of course), and polls.

Google+ posts can be shared publicly, with certain people, or Google+ circles using the To: field in the post dialog box.

### Hangouts

Without a doubt, Hangouts is the most successful aspect of Google+. It's like everything that was great about a late 1990s chat room combined with the power of Skype-like services. A Hangout generates a URL. Participants can use that link to leave and come back to a Hangout at any time, just like a chat room.

You can start a Hangout from inside Google+ or Gmail, or you can use the dedicated Hangouts app. To start a Hangout, you'll enter friends' names (if they're contacts in Google+) or email addresses (if they're not). You can also add entire Google+ circles or make a Hangout open to the entire public. If you'd rather have a private call, though, just add a single name.

Hangouts takes advantage of your Chromebook's built-in microphone and camera, just like Skype or FaceTime. It's easy to use and, as long as you have a free wi-fi connection, completely free.

GMAIL

Gmail is Google's proprietary email client, and we think it's the best of the bunch when it comes to web email hosts. If you've set up a new Google account for your Chromebook, then your Gmail address is your username plus @gmail.com. If you need to check your Gmail account from another computer, visit gmail.com and enter your Google Account username and password to sign in. You can open Gmail in any browser, like Internet Explorer or Firefox.

Opening the Gmail app on your Chromebook will take you straight to your Gmail inbox.

Gmail presorts your mail into three tabs—Primary, Social, and Promotions. This is a great way to tame an unruly inbox. All your Facebook notifications show up under Social, and those daily emails from that store you went to once will appear under Promotions, helping you focus on the email you most likely really want to read.

Of course, occasional mistakes will happen. If a message appears under the wrong tab, just drag it to the tab that you'd like future messages from that sender to appear under.

You'll notice the first time you open Gmail that the Chromebook Gmail app guides you through some basic setup tasks that will help you really get to know Gmail, if you don't already. You can choose a theme, import contacts, work through a tutorial, install Gmail on a mobile phone, and add a new profile image. Take some time and work through these steps—you'll be glad you did and it makes for a great introduction to Gmail.

Sending Email in Gmail

To start a new email message, open Gmail and click the red Compose button in the left menu.

COMPOSE

This brings up the Compose pop-up screen, which allows you to compose your email while keeping an eye on your inbox. Enter the email address of your recipient in the To field and the subject of your email in the Subject field. If you need to add a CC (Carbon Copy, which is visible to other recipients) or BCC (Blind Carbon Copy— invisible to other recipients) recipient, click the gray Cc Bcc text in the top right corner of the New Message window. Then, of course, your message goes in the big blank area. When you're finished writing, click the blue Send button in the lower left corner of the New Message window to send your email.

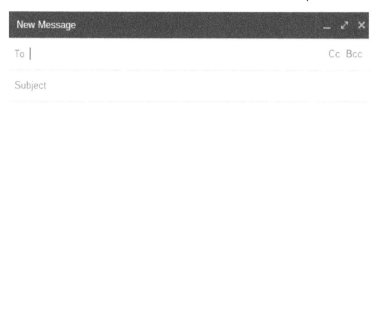

Gmail also makes it easy to format your email and add attachments and multimedia. Next to the Send button, the A icon will display options for formatting text (bold, italics, font choice, etc.). Next, the paper clip icon opens up a dialog box that lets you browse your Chromebook for files to attach to your message, like PDFs, Google Docs documents, etc. If you have a file in Drive that you'd like to insert, use the Drive icon instead of the paper clip. You can use the $ icon as a sort of Google version of PayPal, if you have a credit card or bank account set up in your Google account. The camera icon lets you add images to your email —either as attachments or inside the email itself.

Next, the chain link icon lets you add links to your email. If you type a full website address, like www.google.com, Gmail will recognize the link and will send it as such Finally, you can insert Google emoticons using the smiley face icon.

Gmail saves draft messages for you automatically. If you accidentally close a message you're working on, you'll find it safe and sound in your Drafts folder on the left. However, if you decide you don't want to save a draft message, use the trashcan icon in the lower right corner of the New Message window to delete it.

Inbox (3)

Starred

Sent Mail

Drafts

More ▾

The downward arrow in the far lower right corner of the New Message window gives you a few more options for managing your message. Perhaps the most immediately useful thing here is the spell-check function, but it's good to know how to print a draft or send it to full screen as well. We'll talk about labels in just a minute.

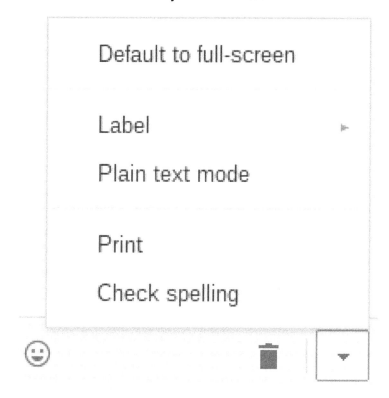

## Managing Email

Gmail makes it exceptionally easy to deal with the daily barrage of incoming messages in this day and age. The toolbar pictured below appears at the top of every email, and will appear when emails are selected in the inbox or a folder.

When you're finished with a message, you can delete it, either from inside the opened message or by clicking the checkbox next to the email in your inbox, and then clicking the trashcan icon. However, Gmail makes it easy to get messages out of your inbox, thus decreasing clutter, without actually deleting them, thanks to its Archive feature. The archive button is the first icon in the Gmail toolbar. When you archive a message, it disappears from your inbox, but not from your account. You can search for it at any time using Gmail's search bar at the top of the Gmail screen.

Of course, sometimes archiving isn't quite nuanced enough, and that's where favorites and labels come in. To make an email a favorite, just click the star icon next to it. You can then get to all of your starred emails by clicking Starred in the left menu.

Labels are an easy way to categorize your email. You can add as many custom labels as you like in the left menu. Just click More in the left menu, and then click Create New Label at the bottom.

COMPOSE

Sent Mail

Drafts

Less ▲

Important

Chats

All Mail

Spam

Trash

▾ Categories

⚇ **Social (1)**

🏷 Promotions

ⓘ Updates

🗫 Forums

Manage labels

Create new label

To apply a label (or labels) to a message, click the Label icon in the top toolbar. A dropdown menu will appear that gives you a list of all of your existing labels. Click on one to apply it, or type in a new label in the box to set it up and add it to the message.

### Contacts

You may have noticed that there's no dedicated contact app in Chromebook. That's because, between Gmail and Google+, there's no real need for one. Gmail is an excellent contacts manager in its own right, and Google+ adds additional contacts capabilities.

To manage contacts in Gmail, click the red Gmail text in the top left corner. A dropdown menu will appear, allowing you to switch to Contacts or Tasks view. All of your Google+ contacts will be automatically added, but you can add non-Google+ information and people as well. To manually add a new contact, click the red New Contact button.

**NEW CONTACT**

You can then add names, pictures, emails, phone numbers, addresses—basically, as much or as little information as you want. To add a field other than the ones displayed, just click the Add button underneath all of the text entry fields. There's plenty to choose from!

↰　　　👥 ▾　　　✉　　　More ▾

Add name

Add a picture　　　☆　My Contacts

Email　　　[                    ]

Phone　　🏳 ▾　[                ]

Address　　　[                    ]

Birthday　　　[                    ]

URL　　　[                    ]

Add ▾

## Chat/Calls

You can start chats and initiate calls from within
Gmail itself. At the very bottom of the left menu,
you'll see three icons—Hangouts, Chats, and
Phone Calls. Click each one to view any contacts
you may have that have these features enabled.
You can start a Hangout (Google's Skype-like video
calling service, covered in more depth later on in
Part 3.8), text-based chat, or phone call by clicking
a contact's name.

Tasks

Much like Microsoft Outlook, Gmail includes a Task list. You can add items to your task list, add new lists altogether, and set due dates. It's a very simple task manager, but like everything else in Gmail, it's accessible from any machine with an Internet browser.

## YOUTUBE

We can't imagine the modern Internet without YouTube. YouTube is very tightly integrated with your Google account, so you're automatically signed in whenever you open the YouTube app.

Watching Videos

Perhaps the most obvious thing you'll want to do with the YouTube app is watch streaming videos online. This is easy and extremely addictive! You can search for videos using the YouTube search bar at the top of the YouTube app page, or you can browse around the featured videos underneath.

When you've found a video you'd like to watch, simply click it in the search results list. It'll start to play. Note that many popular YouTube videos and/or videos that use copyrighted material like songs may play an ad before the video starts. Try not to be too annoyed—this is how YouTube remains free and full of hilarious parodies, remixes, and reinterpretations that make it so much fun!

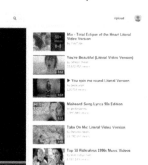

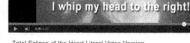

I whip my head to the right!

Total Eclipse of the Heart Literal Video Version

There are media controls in the lower left corner of the YouTube player window where you can pause the video, control the volume, and see the elapsed and remaining time. In the lower right corner, you'll find some additional features, including (from left to right) Watch Later, Settings (where you can adjust the speed and quality of the video playback depending on your system and connection speed), Theatre Mode and Full Screen. Theatre Mode is sort of halfway between the normal YouTube display and Full Screen—try it out to see if it's for you. Full Screen, of course, is the best way to get your computer to mimic a television.

To the right of the video player, you'll see a list of related videos. This is great if you're entertaining yourself with one of the millions of YouTube memes out there (literal music videos, inappropriate music for movies, and Sharky the Pit Bull are some of our classic favorites).

You can thumbs up or thumbs down a video, or comment on it to take advantage of YouTube's social features. Scroll down to see the comments underneath the player. We're not going to lie to you here. YouTube comments can be...rough. We ask in the name of a brighter Internet future that if you're going to participate in YouTube commentary that you 1) don't feed the trolls, and 2) don't be a troll! <u>Trolls</u>, for the record, are Internet users who say inflammatory and frequently extremely offensive things for the purpose of eliciting a reaction, and you're probably going to come across them if you spend much time on the site.

## Account Features

There's more to YouTube than simply browsing around and watching online videos. Using your Google account, you can create playlists of YouTube videos, subscribe to other users' channels, access a list of your recently viewed videos, and create a Watch Later list for when you just don't have time for that twenty minute documentary on urban beekeeping but are really interested. You'll find all of these options in the YouTube menu to the left of the main content area. You can click the menu button next to the YouTube logo in the top left corner to hide and reveal these extra features as needed.

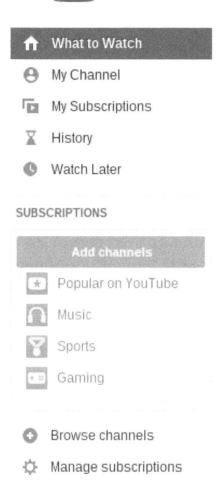

To subscribe to a YouTube channel, locate the channel's owner on a video page, or, if you know the owner's name, just search for it using the YouTube search bar. Then, on their profile page, click the red Subscribe button. You'll then find new content from that user under Subscriptions in the YouTube menu.

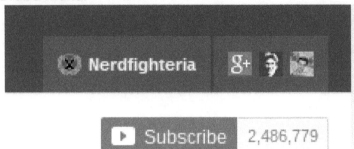

To create a playlist of YouTube videos, click Add to underneath the creators' names on the video's page. Before you can take advantage of this, though, you'll need to set up your Google+ profile and your YouTube channel page. The first time you click Add to you'll be prompted to set all of this up if you haven't already.

# Who I Was in High School

Uploading Videos
If you'd like to upload your own videos to YouTube, just click the Upload button in the top right corner.

You'll need to set up your Google+ profile and your YouTube channel page before you can upload, but after that you can easily upload and share your videos. Videos can be private or only shared with certain people. You can also choose to enable or disable public comments, depending on your preference.

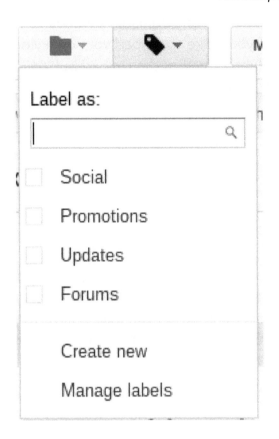

You can click on your labels in the left menu to see all messages categorized with them. You can also search for labels in the Gmail search bar.

CALCULATOR

The Calculator app is a simple utility and a rare example of an app that doesn't open inside a Chrome window. It performs basic calculations—no more, no less. It's nice to have a calculator that appears outside of all your other Chrome tabs and windows, though, and you may want to consider pinning it to your Chromebook's shelf if you find yourself using it time and time again.

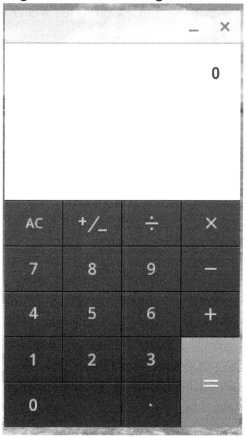

## CAMERA

Most Chromebook devices include at least a forward-facing camera, and the camera app is your go-to for Chromebook or Slate selfie purposes. The Camera app includes several filters to add fun (and sometimes funny) effects to your photos, a timer, and mirroring, which reverses an image so that it would match what you see in the mirror. It's a simple single-action app, but it's great to have when you need a quick snap for a profile pic or message.

CHROME REMOTE DESKTOP

Chrome Remote Desktop (CRD) is similar in function to Windows Remote Desktop and Apple Remote Desktop. Basically, it allows you to view and control a different computer or device remotely. It's incredibly helpful for Instructional Technology (IT) professionals and for getting help with your system.

For Chrome Remote Desktop to work, both machines must be running the CRD app, which can be installed in Chrome in any operating system, as long as the Google Chrome browser is installed. To open a connection, the remote user needs to open the CRD app and click Share. This will generate an access code, which the remote user will give to you. Enter the access code into CRD on your Chromebook, and you'll be able to see and control the remote machine.

GOOGLE+ PHOTOS

The Google+ Photos app is your Chromebook's photo manager. It's not entirely unlike Apple's iPhoto, but it is very tightly integrated with Google+, for better or worse. Google+ Photos helps you consolidate your photos, organize them and share them through Google+.

To get started, open the app using the Apps button. You'll need to sign up for Google+ if you haven't already done so. From there, you can import photos from your Google+ account, your Chromebook, or Google Drive by clicking the Add Photos button in the top right corner. You can then organize your photos into albums, share them through Google+, delete them, or save them to your Chromebook or your Google Drive account.

The Photos app includes the ability to rotate the photo and/or enhance it using the Enhance tool, which appears when you move your mouse over the photo. This is an automatic fix rather than a set of manual features. For serious photo editing, we recommend Pixlr Editor or another photo app from the Web Store.

GOOGLE KEEP

Google Keep is a note-taking app that aims to compete with products like Microsoft OneNote or Evernote. You can add notes and reminders lists that will sync with the online version of Keep at keep.google.com. There's also an Android app that you can download for your smartphone or tablet.

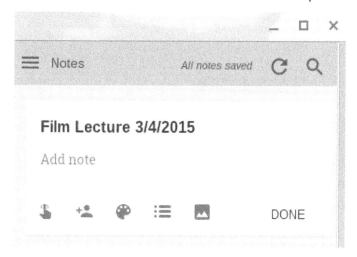

Notes in Keep can include lists and images, and you can share them with others. It's a handy way to keep yourself organized, and it's a quick note-taking app for those times when you don't need all the bells and whistles of Google Docs.

## GOOGLE MAPS AND GOOGLE MY MAPS

Google Maps is, in our opinion, the best free online maps service in the game, and it's built right into your Chromebook.

To use Google Maps, type the address, town or place name (The House on the Rock, Yellowstone National Park, etc.), into the search box in the top left corner. From there, you can get directions to that address by clicking Directions, or you can save the location for later reference. In the example above, you can see that Google Maps also pulled reviews and contact information for us, since we searched for a popular tourist destination.

In the bottom left corner, you will see a box labeled Earth. Clicking this box will toggle Google Earth—a beautiful satellite mode that will give you a photographic aerial view of your mapped area. You can switch back to Map mode by clicking the Map square in the bottom left corner.

In the bottom right corner of the screen, you'll find a few controls for adjusting your Google Maps experience. The Target button is a shortcut to your current location. Click it to get a map of your immediate surroundings. Beneath it, the + and - buttons let you zoom in and out. You can zoom out to a planetary view if you like!

The little yellow man in the controls area is the Google Streetview operator. Drag him from this menu to a spot on the map to enter Streetview. Streetview is a great way to check out a neighborhood or to explore the world a little. The screenshot below is the view from beneath the Eiffel Tower.

## Google My Maps

The Google My Maps app is somewhat confusingly named, but it's extremely useful if you ever need to share directions with a large group of people. It's basically Google Maps, but slightly remixed in such a way that users can save maps in Google Drive and import layers of data into the Maps interface. For example, you might have a spreadsheet listing addresses that you'd like to add. You can also add placemarks and give them your own description or draw lines or add Google Maps routes and directions. Once your custom map is complete, you can share it using a generated link that can be copied and pasted wherever you need it, or through email, Google+, Facebook, and Twitter. This is a very handy feature for invitations or websites.


## GOOGLE FORMS

Google Forms is a form generator that works closely with Google Sheets. If you've ever used Survey Monkey before, you should feel right at home in Forms. Your Forms questions can include multiple choice, text, checkboxes, scales, grids, dates and times, and you can make as many answers required as you like. Once your form is complete, you can invite people to fill it out through a URL or through email invitations. Responses will be automatically recorded in a Google Sheets spreadsheet for analysis (though you can turn this off if you'd prefer to keep all responses inside the Forms app for some reason).

Page 1 of 1

**Board Meeting in March**

Form Description

| | |
|---|---|
| Question Title | Which of the following dates can you attend a board meeting? |
| Help Text | Choose as many dates as you like. |
| Question Type | Multiple choice ▾   Go to page based on answer |

- March 7
- March 21
- March 28

or Add "Other"

▸ Advanced settings

**Done**   ✓ Required question

## GOOGLE DRAWINGS

The Google Drawings app allows you to create and annotate images. You can also insert text boxes, shapes, and lines. The freeform drawing tool is called Scribbles, and you'll find it under Insert > Line. Drawings shouldn't be compared to giants like Photoshop or Illustrator. Its closest relative is probably Microsoft Paint. Of course, any images you create in Drawings are saved in Drive, meaning it's very easy to insert them into other Drive apps, like Google Slides or Google Docs.

## PLAY MUSIC, PLAY BOOKS, AND PLAY MOVIES

These three media apps make it possible to enjoy music, books, and movies purchased from the Google Play Store and from elsewhere on your Chromebook.

### Play Music

The Play Music app includes an optional subscription that gives you access to millions of streaming songs without any ads. First time users generally get some sort of free trial offer, but after that it costs $9.99 a month.

If you decide to use the Standard version of Play Music, you'll then be given the option to upload your music from other sources, including iTunes. To do this, you may need to navigate to Google Play Music from the device that has your tunes on it, which is probably not your relatively low-memory Chromebook. However, once you've uploaded your library (from anywhere), you can enjoy it streaming through Play Music on your Chromebook and on most other devices by installing the Play Music app. You can upload up to 50,000 songs free of charge.

Play Books

Play Books is an ebook app that's half bookshelf and half bookstore. At the top of the Play Books app, you'll see two links—My Books and Shop Books. Any books you've purchased through the Shop link (or through the Google Play Store on a different computer) will appear under My Books. Buying books is identical to buying apps or extensions. If you don't already have a credit card number on file with Google, you'll be prompted to enter one. Of course, there are a number of classics and other free titles in the Play Store, so there's no need to whip out the plastic if you don't want to!

Any books you buy through Play Books will be available on your Android smartphone or tablet as well, and the Play Books app will keep everything synced up. This means that no matter what device you're using to read, your current read will open to exactly where you left off.

Play Movies

The Play Movies app allows you to enjoy movies and television shows purchased through the Google Play Store. Just like the Play Books app, Play Movies includes a Shop link where you can find streaming video to watch.

Google Play movies and television shows can be bought (you can stream them as many times as you like) or rented (you can only stream them during a certain amount of time). There are often pretty good deals on the Play Store—for example, at the time of writing, Star Trek was on offer in HD for just $4.99.

Star Trek
May 2009
Action & Adventure

$17.99 $4.99 Buy HD    $2.99 Rent    ⊞ Add to Wishlist

★ ★ ★ ★ ☆ (👤 6,645)    8+1 +2851 Recommend this on Google

## GOOGLE CALENDAR

Google Calendar is a great calendar tool, particularly since it's so widely used and importable into a variety of other calendaring systems. It's easy to use, available through google.com/calendar on any computer with a web browser, and will notify you of upcoming events so you never miss a thing.

### Adding a New Calendar Event
To add a new event to Google Calendar, click the red Create button in the top left corner.

CREATE ▼

Enter as much or as little information about your event as you need. Keep in mind that Google Calendar has some powerful time management features to help keep you on track. It will send notifications before your event, at an interval of your choosing. You can also set recurring events by clicking the "Repeat" checkbox.

## Adding and Sharing Calendars

The Google Calendar system includes the ability to set up multiple calendars. Maybe you'd like to have one personal calendar and then a shared family calendar or a team project calendar. To add a new calendar, click the boxed downward pointing arrow to the right of the My Calendars heading in the left menu. This will take you to the New Calendar setup screen. At the bottom, you'll see options for controlling your calendar's privacy and inviting people to view and/or add to the calendar.

## Hiding Calendars

We've found that it's very easy to get enthusiastic about calendars, only to find yourself drowning in calendar entries. Fortunately, it's easy to temporarily hide calendars to help clean up your view. To hide a calendar, just click the little colored square next to its name in the My Calendars list. This won't delete anything, but it will hide all events associated with that calendar so you can focus on the events that need your attention.

# [7]

# MAKING IT YOUR OWN WITH CUSTOMIZATIONS

This chapter will cover:
- Changing the Appearance
- Device
- Searching
- People
- Date and Time
- Privacy
- Web Content
- Languages
- Downloads
- HTTPS/SSL Certificates
- Google Cloud Print
- Startup
- Powerwash and Reset
- Supervised Accounts
- Troubleshooting
- 

If you already have the watch, then you can skip right ahead to the next chapter. How's that for ridiculously simple?! This chapter is just for readers curious about all the different watches available.

The Apple Watch comes in several different.

In this section, we'll talk about several ways you can customize your Chromebook to suit your unique needs and personality. There are quite a few useful tweaks available for Chromebook, and we'll walk you through them all here. We'll also show you how to manage user accounts on your Chromebook, including children's accounts, and give you a few tips for troubleshooting and finding help.

To open your Chromebook settings, click the area of the screen that displays the time, wireless connection, battery, and your profile picture in the bottom right corner. Then click Settings. We're going to examine each heading that appears on this screen.

## CHANGING THE APPEARANCE

The Appearance heading in Settings covers, well, the appearance of your Chromebook. Here you can set your desktop wallpaper to a custom image by clicking Set Wallpaper. This will open up a dialog box where you can browse your Chromebook for the image file you'd like to use. You can also click the Get Themes button to be taken to the Themes area of the Chrome Web Store. Themes add a graphic layer to your Chrome window—an image or color for new tab windows and colors and designs for the menu area. There are plenty of fun themes to choose from, and if you change your mind about any of them, you can always click Reset to Default Theme to go back to Chrome's original appearance.

Appearance

| Set wallpaper... | Get themes | Reset to default theme |

☑ Show Home button

gadchick.com/  Change

☐ Always show the bookmarks bar

You can also set a home page here if you like. First, click Show Home button to tell Chrome to show the Home button in your Chrome browser as a special shortcut to your home page. Click Change to add a new home page. This is the page that will be displayed every time you open Chrome.

Finally, you can choose to always show the bookmarks bar in Chrome here as well.

## DEVICE

The Device heading is a pretty important Settings area, even if it's a little bit of a catchall. There are some really useful options and features tucked away here.

Device

Change settings specific to your device and peripherals.

| Battery... | Stored data... |

Touchpad speed:

| Touchpad settings | Keyboard settings | Display settings |

First, you can take a look at what's using your battery by clicking the Battery button. This is a great way to maximize your Chromebook's battery even further if you need to. Just close the apps that are sucking up the most juice.

The Stored Data button is also a fascinating glimpse into what Chrome is doing with every page and app you visit or use. Check out what our Chromebook has to say about weather.com.

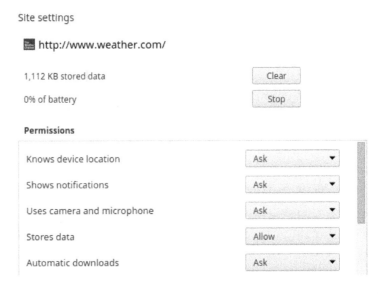

We can see how much stored data from this site is eating into our hard disc (in this case, not very much), as well as how much of the battery it's using. Right now, it's not running, so it requires 0% of our battery. Then we can see a fairly extensive list of permissions for the site, and change them as we see fit. For this example, we may want to allow this site to know our Chromebook's location so that it will always give us the weather of our current spot.

Underneath the battery and stored data information, you'll find some options for configuring your touchpad, keyboard, and display. You can adjust your touchpad's speed to match that of your fingers using the slider, and you can also change the direction the page moves when you scroll and enable or disable tap-to-click. By clicking Keyboard, you can view the shortcut display mentioned earlier in the book, and you can also change the behavior of certain keyboard keys if you like—namely Search, CTRL, and ALT.

Keyboard settings ×

Search    Search    ▼

Ctrl    Ctrl    ▼

Alt    Alt    ▼

☐ Treat top-row keys as function keys

Hold the Search key to switch the behavior of the top-row keys.

☑ Enable auto-repeat

Delay before repeat:    Long    Short

Repeat rate:    Slow    Fast

View keyboard shortcuts

Change language and input settings

OK    Cancel

SEARCHING

One of our favorite things about Google products is their flexibility. It would stand to reason that the proprietary Google OS based on Google's browser would limit users to the Google search engine for the Chrome omnibox, but that's not the case. In the Search heading, you can change Chrome's search engine to Yahoo!, Bing, Ask, or AOL.

Search

Set which search engine is used when searching from the omnibox.

Google ▼ | Manage search engines...

The Manage Search Engines button finds additional search engines, like YouTube search, for example. You can add these highly specific searches as your omnibox default if you'd like (though for most users we do recommend sticking with a general internet-wide search engine).

## PEOPLE

Under the People heading, you can accomplish two important tasks. First, you can manage what aspects of your Chromebook sync with your Google Account by clicking Advanced Sync Settings. By default, everything is selected, but you can adjust as needed. You can also choose how you'd like Google Chrome to encrypt your data.

The other feature under People is the ability to manage logins on your Chromebook. More than one Google user can sign in, and you can manage other users as needed. You can decide whether or not to enable a Guest account and supervised users (which we'll talk about in more detail shortly) and whether or not to restrict sign-in to certain users. You can also add users to your Chromebook here.

At this point, you'll need to click Show Advanced Settings to see the rest of the Chrome settings menu!

## DATE AND TIME

There's not much here besides the ability to change your time zone and switch your system clock to 24-hour time. Chrome will set the date and time automatically based on your time zone.

Date and time

Time zone:    (UTC-6:00) Central Standard Time (Chicago)      ▼

☐ Use 24-hour clock

Date and time are set automatically.

## PRIVACY

Your privacy settings give you some control over how much information your Chromebook shares with the rest of the world. Google uses quite a few prediction services in order to load pages fast and get you where you want to go, but you may not want all of them accessing your personal information, search engine terms, etc. To disable any of these services, deselect them under the Privacy heading.

The Content settings button includes several Chrome options, like pop-up blocking, location tracking, JavaScript settings, automatic downloads and more. Most of these settings include a Manage exceptions button. As you surf the web, Chrome will ask you if you'd like to make these exceptions. For example, when Chrome blocks a pop-up, it will notify you of the action and then ask if you'd like to allow pop-ups once or always for that site. You can then revoke those exceptions later if you need to in Content Settings.

Generally we recommend leaving these settings with their defaults, as we think there's a good balance between end-user protection and convenience of use. Nevertheless, you may occasionally need to turn off the pop-up blocker or adjust another one of these settings, and it's good to know where to find them.

WEB CONTENT

The web content settings allow you to change the default font size and page zoom for web pages. You can also choose what sort of font you'd like Chrome to display as a default.

LANGUAGES

The Languages heading allows you to turn automatic translation offers on and off. You can also manage the languages you'd like to use with Chromebook by clicking the Language and input settings button. You can add more than one by clicking the Add button in the lower left corner. The language at the top of your list will be your default language, but adding additional languages gives you the ability to set up keyboard input options so that you can quickly switch languages as needed.

Languages and Input            ×

Add languages and drag to order them based on your preference. For text input, select a language to see available input methods. Learn more

| Languages | Chinese (Simplified) - 中文（简体中文） |
|---|---|
| English (United States) | Display Google Chrome in this language |
| English | This language cannot be used for spell checking |
| Spanish (Latin America) | ☐ Offer to translate pages in this language |
| Chinese (Simplified)    × | **Input Method** |
| | ☐ Pinyin input method |
| | ☐ Wubi input method |

Add

Press Alt+Shift to switch between input methods.
Press Ctrl+Space to select the previous input method.
Custom spelling dictionary

Done

# DOWNLOADS

Here you can change the way your Chromebook handles downloads. Perhaps the most useful feature here is the ability to change the default downloads location to something more accessible than the Downloads folder. Or, if you prefer, you can tell Chrome that you want it to always ask you where you want to save downloads. You can disable Google Drive here as well, though we don't recommend it.

Downloads

Download location: Downloads     [ Change... ]

☐ Ask where to save each file before downloading

☐ Disable Google Drive on this device

## HTTPS/SSL CERTIFICATES

This area of your settings allows you to view and manage security certificates stored on your computer. The average user won't have too many reasons to make changes here, but it's good to know it's there if you're ever prompted to install or uninstall a certificate.

## GOOGLE CLOUD PRINT

Google Cloud Print is Google's printing service. It allows users to send a print job over the web to their printer, rather than the traditional methods of wired or wireless printer connections. To use it, you'll need to connect your printer to your Google Cloud Print account. You'll find instructions and more information about this by clicking Learn more under the Google Cloud Print heading.

## STARTUP

The On Startup heading tells Chrome what to do the first time you open it. You can start with a new tab page, or open the pages that you had open during your last use (the default option). You can also set a page or group of pages that you'd like to open. This is a great way to open your email, Facebook, the news, and your favorite blog without having to do anything but start Google Chrome.

On startup

○ Open the New Tab page

● Continue where you left off

○ Open a specific page or set of pages.  Set pages

## POWERWASH AND RESET

The powerwash and reset options are located at the very bottom of the advanced settings screen. Powerwash is the panic button. This extreme step will completely erase everything on your Chromebook and restore it to factory settings. It can be used as an absolutely last-ditch troubleshooting measure, but just remember that it's permanent—there's no recovering from a Powerwash (though of course you can re-download anything you've purchased through Google, and since almost everything on Chromebook is a web app, you won't lose any of your files stored in Google Drive). Powerwash is also the thing to do if you're selling or giving away your Chromebook.

A less drastic approach is the Reset button. This doesn't wipe your device, but it does restore all system settings to their original defaults. If you've played with your configuration and decided you prefer the original, just hit Reset to get back to square one without losing your apps or data.

## SUPERVISED ACCOUNTS

If you have any children in your house, you may want to set up supervised accounts for them. This will allow them to use your Chromebook, but with a few restrictions designed to keep them safe and you sane. You can restrict web pages and content for supervised users, and you can log in anytime to chrome.com/manage to monitor the account.

To add a supervised user, click Add user on the sign-in screen. A sign-in box will appear. Click Create a supervised user (in blue) on the right side of the box to get started.

Next, you'll name the account and set a password and profile picture. Supervised users aren't Google Accounts users, so there's no need to set up a unique username. You can also set a password that's easy to remember, since it's for a local account instead of an online one.

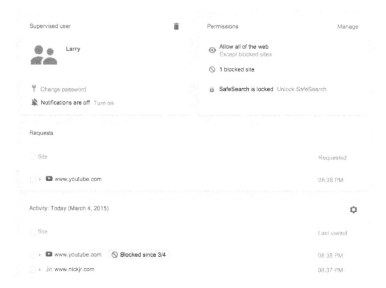

At chrome.com/manage, you can change the supervised user's password, set restricted sites, and deal with requests to unblock sites from the user, as seen above.


## TROUBLESHOOTING AND MAINTAINING YOUR CHROMEBOOK

One of the best things about Chromebook is its simplicity—unlike more complex operating system software like Windows or Mac OSX, there's really very little that can go wrong. However, things can and do happen sometimes, and we'll walk you through some quick and easy troubleshooting methods here.

### Check Your Battery

Also known as the "is it plugged in?" step, this is a frequent culprit in Chromebook problems. Check to be sure that your charger is connected and plugged in before you jump to any conclusions as to why your Chromebook won't wake up.

### Restart

When in doubt, reboot. This often is all it takes to fix frozen systems or other irritating problems. Thanks to most Chrome apps' constant background saving processes, you rarely need to worry about losing work when you do this.

If you're having problems with an app, you can always try closing it and reopening it. If that doesn't work, you may want to try removing it from your device and then re-downloading it from the Web Store.

### Getting Help and Contacting Support

If you're stuck with a Chromebook problem, try the Get Help app. It's a searchable tour of your Chromebook's features and may provide the answer you need. If that doesn't work, you might try the Google user forums at https:// support.google.com chromebook-central. Here you'll find frequently asked questions, user forums where you can search for other people with your issue (or post it yourself), and more. You'll find power Google users to be a pretty informed bunch, and the forums are an excellent resource when you run into trouble.

To get official support for your Chromebook, you can either request a call or start a chat session with a Google technician. To do this, visit support.google.com/Chromebook and click Contact Us in the top right corner.

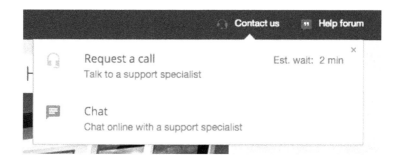

## Updating Your Chromebook

Chromebook keeps itself up-to-date for the most part, so the only thing you need to do is be sure that it's regularly online and in use. Chrome will take care of the rest! If you ever need to see what version of Chrome you're running, you can do so by visiting Chrome Settings. Then click About Chrome OS at the top. This will display your device's update status, as well as its current version.

It's a good idea to periodically check that your system is updating itself. You may occasionally need to click Check for and apply updates to manually perform an update check. Sometimes new updates require a system restart, fortunately, most Chromebooks restart within seconds!

# APPENDIX A: SPECS

| Specification | Pixelbook | Surface Laptop | MacBook |
|---|---|---|---|
| Software | Chrome OS | Windows 10 S | macOS High Sierra |
| Display | 12.3 inches | 13.5 inches | 12 inches |
| Resolution | 2400 x 1600 | 2256 x 1504 | 2304 x 1440 |
| Processor (base) | Intel Core i5 (seventh-gen) | Intel Core i5 (seventh-gen) | Intel Core m3 (1.2GHz, dual-core, seventh-gen) |
| Processor (max) | Intel Core i7 (seventh-gen) | Intel Core i7 (seventh-gen) | Intel Core i7 (1.4GHz, dual-core, seventh-gen) |

| RAM (base) | 8GB | 4GB | 8GB |
|---|---|---|---|
| RAM(max) | 16GB | 16GB | 16GB |
| Ports | USB-C, 3.5mm headphone jack | USB 3.0, 3.5mm headphone jack, Mini DisplayPort | USB-C, 3.5mm headphone jack |
| Storage | 128GB, 256GB, 512GB | 128GB, 256GB, 512GB, 1TB | 256GB, 512GB |
| Weight | 2.4 pounds | 2.76 pounds | 2.03 pounds |
| Starting price | $999 | $999 | $1,299 |

# APPENDIX B: SHORTCUT KEYS

## Popular shortcuts

- Open the Google Assistant: Press [⬚]

- Search your device, apps, web and more: Press [⬚]

- Open the status area (where your account picture appears): Press [≡]

- Take a screenshot: Press Ctrl + [⬚]

- Take a partial screenshot: Press Ctrl + Shift + [⬚] , then click and drag

- Turn Caps Lock on or off: Press Alt + Search

- Lock your screen: Press Search + L

- Sign out of your Google Account: Press Ctrl + Shift + q (twice)

-

## All other shortcuts

Note: If you're using a Windows or Mac keyboard, use the Windows key or Command key in place of the Search key.

# Tabs and windows

| | |
|---|---|
| Open a new window | Ctrl + n |
| Open a new window in incognito mode | Ctrl + Shift + n |
| Open a new tab | Ctrl + t |
| Open a file in the browser | Ctrl + o |
| Close the current tab | Ctrl + w |
| Close the current window | Ctrl + Shift + w |
| Reopen the last tab or window you closed | Ctrl + Shift + t |
| Go to tabs 1-8 in the window | Ctrl + 1 through Ctrl + 8 |
| Go to the last tab in the window | Ctrl + 9 |
| Go to the next tab in the window | Ctrl + Tab |
| Go to the previous tab in the window | Ctrl + Shift + Tab |
| Switch quickly between windows | Press & hold Alt, tap Tab until you get to the window you want to open, then release. |

| | |
|---|---|
| Open the window you used least recently | Press & hold Alt + Shift, tap Tab until you get to the window you want to open, then release. |
| Go to previous page in your browsing history | Alt + left arrow |
| Go to the next page in your browsing history | Alt + right arrow |
| Open the link in a new tab in the background | Press Ctrl and click a link |
| Open the link in a new tab and switch to the new tab | Press Ctrl + Shift and click a link |
| Open the link in a new window | Press Shift and click a link |
| Open the link in the tab | Drag the link to the tab's address bar |
| Open the link in a new tab | Drag the link to a blank area on the tab strip |
| Open the webpage in a new tab | Type a web address (URL) in the address bar, then press Alt + Enter |

| | |
|---|---|
| Return the tab to its original position | While dragging the tab, press Esc |
| Dock a window on the left | Alt + [ |
| Dock a window on the right | Alt + ] |

## Page & Web Browser

| | |
|---|---|
| Page up | Alt or Search and up arrow |
| Page down | Alt or Search and down arrow |
| Scroll down the web page | Space bar |
| Go to top of page | Ctrl + Alt and up arrow |
| Go to bottom of page | Ctrl + Alt and down arrow |
| Print your current page | Ctrl + p |
| Save your current page | Ctrl + s |
| Reload your current page | Ctrl + r |
| Reload your current page without using cached content | Ctrl + Shift + r |
| Zoom in on the page | Ctrl and + |
| Zoom out on the page | Ctrl and - |
| Reset zoom level | Ctrl + 0 |
| Stop the loading of your current page | Esc |
| Right-click a link | Press Alt and click a link |
| Open the link in a new tab in the background | Press Ctrl and click a link |

| | |
|---|---|
| Save the link as a bookmark | Drag link to bookmarks bar |
| Save your current webpage as a bookmark | Ctrl + d |
| Save all open pages in your current window as bookmarks in a new folder | Ctrl + Shift + d |
| Search the current page | Ctrl + f |
| Go to the next match for your search | Ctrl + g or Enter |
| Go to the previous match for your search | Ctrl + Shift + g or Shift + Enter |
| Perform a Google search | ☐ or Ctrl + k or Ctrl + e |
| Add www. and .com to your input in the address bar, then open the page | Ctrl + Enter |
| View page source | Ctrl + u |
| Show or hide the Developer Tools panel | Ctrl + Shift + i |
| Show or hide the DOM Inspector | Ctrl + Shift + j |
| Show or hide the bookmarks bar | Ctrl + Shift + b |

| | |
|---|---|
| Open the History page | Ctrl + h |
| Open the Downloads page | Ctrl + j |

## System & Display Settings

| | |
|---|---|
| Open the Files app | Alt + Shift + m |
| Preview a file in the Files app | Select the file, then press Space |
| Display hidden files in the Files app | Ctrl + . |
| Open the status area (where your account picture appears) | [≡] or Shift + Alt + s |
| Click icons 1-8 on your shelf | Alt + 1 through Alt + 8 |
| Click the last icon on your shelf | Alt + 9 |
| Use F keys (F1 to F12) | Search + 1 through Search + = |
| See your notifications | Alt + Shift + n |
| Change screen resolution | Ctrl + Shift and + or - |
| Reset screen resolution to default | Ctrl + Shift + 0 |
| Rotate screen 90 degrees | Ctrl + Shift + [↻] |
| Switch to the next user | Ctrl + Alt + . |
| Switch to the previous user | Ctrl + Alt + , |

## Text Editing

| | |
|---|---|
| Turn Caps Lock on or off | Alt + Search |
| Select everything on the page | Ctrl + a |
| Select the content in the address bar | Ctrl + L or Alt + d |
| Select the next word or letter | Ctrl + Shift and right arrow |
| Select text to the end of the line | Shift + Search and right arrow |
| Select text to the beginning of the line | Shift + Search and left arrow |
| Select previous word or letter | Ctrl + Shift and left arrow |
| Move to the end of the next word | Ctrl and right arrow |
| Move to the start of the previous word | Ctrl and left arrow |
| Go to end of document | Ctrl + Search and right arrow |
| Go to beginning of document | Ctrl + Search and left arrow |
| Copy selected content to the clipboard | Ctrl + c |
| Paste content from the clipboard | Ctrl + v |

| | |
|---|---|
| Paste content from the clipboard as plain text | Ctrl + Shift + v |
| Cut | Ctrl + x |
| Delete the previous word | Ctrl + Backspace |
| Delete the next letter (forward delete) | Alt + Backspace |
| Undo your last action | Ctrl + z |
| Redo your last action | Ctrl + Shift + z |
| Switch between the keyboard languages you've set. Learn how to choose your keyboard language. | Ctrl + Shift + Space |
| Switch to the previous keyboard language you were using. Learn how to choose your keyboard language. | Ctrl + Space |
| Dim keyboard (for backlit keyboards only) | Alt + ☼ |
| Make keyboard brighter (for backlit keyboards only) | Alt + ☼ |

## Accessibility

Learn how to make your Pixelbook accessible.

| | |
|---|---|
| Turn ChromeVox (spoken feedback) on or off | Ctrl + Alt + z |

| | |
|---|---|
| Turn on high contrast mode | Ctrl + Search + h |
| Highlight the launcher button on your shelf | Shift + Alt + L |
| Highlight the next item on your shelf | Shift + Alt + L, then Tab or right arrow |
| Highlight the previous item on your shelf | Shift + Alt + L, then Shift + Tab or left arrow |
| Open the highlighted button on your shelf | Shift + Alt + L, then Space or Enter |
| Remove the highlight from a button on your shelf | Shift + Alt + L, then Esc |

Switch focus between:

Ctrl + [ ← ]

- Status area (where your account picture appears)

- Launcher

- Address bar

- Bookmarks bar (if visible)

- The webpage that's open

- Downloads bar (if visible)

Highlight the bookmarks bar (if shown)    Alt + Shift + b

Highlight the row with the address bar    Shift + Alt + t

Open right-click menu for highlighted item    Shift + [ • ]